YOU'RE KIDDING, RIGHT?

One Local Church's Journey Into the Miraculous

by

Eva Boyd Evans, Ph.D., Th.D., D.Div.

Copyright © 2004 by Eva Boyd Evans, Ph.D,Th.D, D.Div.

You're Kidding, Right?
by Eva Boyd Evans, Ph.D,Th.D, D.Div.

Printed in the United States of America

ISBN 1-594673-63-2

All rights reserved by the author. The contents and views expressed in this book are solely those of the author and are not necessarily those of Xulon Press, Inc. The author guarantees this book is original and does not infringe upon any laws or rights, and that this book is not libelous, plagiarized or in any other way illegal. If any portion of this book is fictitious, the author guarantees it does not represent any real event or person in a way that could be deemed libelous. No part of this book may be reproduced in any form without the permission of the author.

Dedication

This book is lovingly dedicated to my Grandson,
Ryan Elijah Evans, whose generation will finally get it right.

Foreword

In 1981, Cornerstone was established to help encircle the city of Washington, DC, with the Gospel and the Love and Works of Jesus Christ. Charismatic by birth, we knew that nothing short of miracles would touch the area and the generation to whom we would give our lives. We set the church in order, established a bible college and began to feed the hungry and care for the poor. Gifted people were added to us and soon the vision became corporate.

From the beginning, we DID see miracles:
- A woman was given a complete new heart. Doctors' reports before and after verify this miracle.
- A broken arm was instantly healed.
- A baby girl was given no chance to live at birth. Within two hours prayer had changed everything, and two days later she went home with her happy parents.
- An inoperable brain tumor disappeared.

- A woman born with clubfeet and who had undergone numerous surgeries was healed in a Sunday morning service and was able to walk.
- A young woman who was five weeks pregnant was brought back from the dead and gave birth to a perfect baby girl eight months later.

It was the miracles, the changed lives and the daily awareness of the power of the Gospel that kept us going. We were always looking for the next miracle and that flood of revival that would change the world. Little did we know that we would experience things that we could never have anticipated.

There are many other testimonies of healings and miracles that took place during that time period.

Note to the Readers

It is important to us that you understand that the events in this book are absolutely, accurately reported. Although we may not use complete names of persons or places, all of the miracles are documented in the Archives of Cornerstone. Many of the healings also have doctors' verifications, and almost all were witnessed by numbers of people, including Cornerstone staff. Almost all are first-person accounts.

Chapter 1

In 1998, we began to hear about the gold miracles in South America. I had read in historic accounts of the ancient church that gold dust would sometimes appear on martyrs and on the clothes and faces of living people or holy objects.

We first saw the gold dust at Calvary Pentecostal Tabernacle in Ashland, Virginia. I believe that is the first place in America to experience gold dust, and it was disbursed from there to many places in this nation. The late Ruth Ward Heflin (known to the world as Sister Ruth) was Director at that time, and it was amazing to see how the gold would appear. She would come into the service looking like everyone else. Soon, she would start to sparkle, and in a little while the gold dust was on her face, arms, hands and clothing. The chairs on the platform sparkled, as did the carpet, and usually anyone sitting on the platform and many people in the audience would experience this wonder. Anyone who saw the gold knew it was real because there was no way it could have been faked. I have seen it fall like raindrops, but most of the time it just appeared.

We have also experienced the gold dust from time to time in our services at Cornerstone, and some of those events I will recount later.

My family was blessed in a very unusual way. I was sitting with Sister Ruth one evening in a glorious service, and the gold dust seemed to be everywhere. When it was time to take the offering, I picked up my purse, unzipped it and took out my wallet (which also was closed with a zipper). There was no gold dust on my purse or on the outside of my wallet. When I opened the wallet to take out my checkbook, there was gold dust on the checkbook and also inside my wallet where the checkbook had been. I showed it to Sister Ruth and she prophesied to me that it was a sign that my family would have unusual financial miracles. For almost 2 weeks, the gold appeared on my checkbook and inside my wallet. Once, a grocery checker asked me what the glitter was. I replied that it was gold dust and she started to laugh; we both stood there laughing like we knew the funniest thing. Within 10 months of the night Sister Ruth prophesied to me, my family was completely debt free!

I love this next story because of the place where it occurred. I was in a Wednesday evening service at a church in the beautiful White Mountains of New Hampshire. The Presence of Jesus was so real…people were being touched, and everyone became so excited when gold dust appeared on some of the young people. We prayed for healing for several people, including the Grandmother of a young woman named Tea. Her Grandmother was confined to a wheelchair and Tea heard that the next morning she had stood up and danced. Before going to her job at the local Burger King, Tea went to visit her Grandmother. Later that day while on her lunch hour, Tea's supervisor came and asked her to come to the back with her. In Tea's own words, "My supervisor yelled at me for wearing glitter makeup when I knew it was against the rules and told me to go wash it off." Puzzled, Tea went to the restroom and looked in the mirror – she realized she was wearing beautiful gold dust! A few months later, the gold dust began to appear in the youth meetings of that New Hampshire church and has since sparked revival.

I have talked to many people about gold dust. It always seems to elate and encourage and be received as a sign of God's love. The following event would certainly indicate that it was sent to encourage. One of the churches that Cornerstone planted had outgrown its small facility and was ready to begin a school. There was a beautiful property of 91 acres with two usable buildings that we had been praying about for several years. While on a visit to the church, I was walking and praying with the pastor on the property, and I felt that I received very clear directions during the prayer. I told the pastor he should make an appointment with the landowners, tell them we were ready to buy the land, and ask them to give us their price. Then I told him he was to come to Fairfax (over 600 miles away) and meet with our elders. They would know how we were to raise the money. He reluctantly agreed, met with the landowners, and a few days later came to Fairfax. I told the elders how important this meeting was and asked them to fast and pray. Just before the meeting, I had a call that one of the elders would not be able to come because he had to work late. We had barely prayed and opened the meeting when another elder was called away. There were numerous interruptions: One person was offended by something someone said, someone had brought food and there was constant coming and going between the kitchen and the meeting room. The pastor made his presentation and laid out all the facts. Following that, everyone went back to eating and talking, and no one proposed a resolution to the problem. Later, when I was driving him back to his motel, he said he felt like he had wasted his time and wondered what he would tell the landowners. I was very disappointed that the meeting had not accomplished what I had hoped, but I tried to hide my feelings and told him we should wait a few days. Later, at home when I went to clean my face, just below my eye there was a beautiful gold flake. About ten days later at the end of a Sunday morning service, two of our elders told me they were going to buy the land.

Shortly after that, I remembered something that had happened about five years earlier. This same pastor was in town and came to a mid-week service. He was prayed for and fell on the floor. While he was lying there, one of the elders who had prayed for him had a vision of him walking, and every place he stepped he left gold sparkles. When she told him the vision, he laughed and said, "You've been watching too much Disney on TV." This was long before the gold dust had appeared anywhere.

    Jesus Christ never changes. If you will let your faith touch Him, the miracles you are reading about will happen to you!

Chapter 2

In early March of 1999, some of our young people were attending a conference at Toronto Airport Christian Fellowship in Canada. I received a phone call in which five of them were trying to talk at once about the conference. Ordinary tooth fillings had turned gold through prayer and the laying on of hands. They had seen these gold fillings with their own eyes, and pictures of this miraculous happening had been posted on the church's web site. We downloaded the pictures and began to feel very sure that this could happen to us, as well.

My first opportunity to talk about the gold fillings was at a Tuesday night seminary class. At the beginning of the class, I shared what had occurred at the conference and passed around the pictures from the Toronto Airport Christian Fellowship website. Our kids had given detailed descriptions of how the prayer was done and how mouths were checked to determine if the miracle had happened. I explained all of this to the class and asked if they would like to pray for gold fillings. A couple of students looked like they wanted to hide under their desks. I must admit, the atmosphere was not charged with faith or expectation, but I was determined. I was very careful to do everything right. Nothing happened, and I went ahead with the lecture.

I was out of town the next three days. When I returned home late Friday night, I checked my voice mail and there was a message from Kathleen, one of the students. Her message was as follows: "Dr. Eva, I'm sorry to bother you, but I thought you'd like to know that all eight of my dark fillings have turned to gold." It was much too late to return her call, and needless to say, sleep was not easy. My first question when I reached her was:

"What were you doing? Were you praying?"

"No."

"Were you praising?"

"No."

"Were you reading the Bible?"

"No"

"What exactly were you doing, Kathleen?"

"I was riding in my car with my decorator and we were talking about the plans for my house. I felt something strange in my mouth, I pulled off the road and looked and my fillings were gold!"

I told her to make an appointment with her dentist to have him verify that the fillings were gold and that he hadn't used gold in the original fillings.

We were beginning special weekend meetings with an out of town speaker, and I asked Kathleen to please come to the Saturday night service so we could see this miracle. I spent all day Saturday singing, "Eight gold fillings!" Good news does travel fast, and we had excellent attendance on Saturday night. Kathleen was the center of attention, and she graciously let anyone look in her mouth who wanted to do so...it was a marvelous sight. At the proper place in the service, she shared her testimony and then we prayed for tooth miracles. Nothing happened.

Our guest was with us again on Sunday morning, and it was a wonderful service. Toward the end of the service, I spoke briefly about the gold, and we ended by praying for tooth miracles. Nothing happened.

I arrived a little early for the Sunday evening service which we shared with a wonderful Charismatic Episcopal congregation. The worship team was practicing and people were already gathering. Near the front of the church I noticed Cornerstone members Karen, her sister Ann, and Ann's husband Al, very engrossed in conversation. When they saw me they beckoned for me to come over. I noticed that Karen was holding a small flashlight and a dental mirror. She told me that that afternoon she was coloring her hair, and while she was waiting for the color to set, she decided to look at her teeth to see if anything had happened. She thought her dark fillings had gotten much lighter, and she asked me to check them. I thought they were gold, but I asked Al and Ann to look just to make sure. They also thought the fillings were gold, and within a few minutes both Al and Ann had gold fillings too! I cannot express the excitement I felt and in just minutes, the place was buzzing. The praise was glorious and at the proper time, we talked about what had happened to Karen, Ann and Al. We then explained how we were going to pray and how mouths should be checked. We had hardly finished praying when two men came forward and opened their mouths to show that they each had a beautiful gold crown. That evening, twenty-one people received gold in their mouths, either crowns or fillings.

A Cornerstone person named Shelly came forward with her two-year-old nephew and said he had never been to a dentist. He had beautiful white teeth and on his back molar, there was a beautiful ornate gold cross. I asked her later what the boy's mother thought of the miracle. She said the mother lived in crack house, and she wouldn't tell her for fear she'd scrape it off and sell it. I have often wondered what that little boy's life will be like when he's grown.

In all my years of attending church, I had never experienced anything like that Sunday evening service. Everyone was excited. People were standing on chairs to look into mouths and everyone was talking at once. I believe that was a small glimpse of what it must have been like around Jesus when He was ministering. There was a line of people in the office waiting to phone family and friends to tell them to come to the church. I remember seeing a mother standing in the back of the sanctuary wearing a coat over her pajamas and holding on to small children, also in pajamas. A man who had cancer was carried in for prayer.

Jesus Christ never changes. If you will let your faith touch Him, the miracles you are reading about will happen to you!

Chapter 3

The week following the glorious Sunday evening service was spent hearing wonderful testimonies. We also instructed everyone who got gold in their mouths to make an appointment with their dentist to verify that the dentist had not done the work and to evaluate the gold. We heard from many dentists that the gold seemed to be a much higher quality than they would use.

A visitor to the Sunday evening service named Rose had been brought by her neighbor. She had seen some of the gold fillings and had taken part in the excitement. Early on Monday morning, the neighbor's phone rang and when she answered it, she heard crying. It was Rose, and she had just discovered that her dark fillings had turned gold. She insisted that her dentist see her that day. These were her exact words, "The dentist did not seem at all skeptical of my thinking that it was a miracle because of the beauty of the gold."

A neighbor had also brought Mary, another visitor to the Sunday evening service. Mary had been prophesied to early in the service, and she fell on the floor. She was there for a long time, and I remember thinking that I should go ask her if she wanted help getting up, but I never got to her. When she was brushing her teeth before going to bed that night, she found that her dark fillings had turned gold. She had to wait a few days to see her dentist. He asked why she went to another dentist to have the gold fillings done and then come to him to verify it. She told him that she didn't go to another dentist, it had happened in church. He told her she'd better leave that church because only Satan did that kind of thing. She told me, "I knew Satan did not do that because from the night I laid on the floor at Cornerstone, I stopped smoking (three packs a day), I stopped worrying and cussing, and for the first time in years I'm sleeping through the night!" I heard later that she shows her gold fillings everywhere she goes and says, "Look what God did for me!"

The bible college had a Tuesday evening class that was held at a nearby church. The teacher was not able to be there, so we sent a student to monitor a video class. Some people from that church had been in the Sunday night service. They wanted to hear about the gold and wanted to pray to receive it. The student was a little nervous, but she prayed and there was great expectation. Immediately after the prayer, several people had gold fillings. One was Lynn, the church's worship leader. She was so excited that when she got home, she called her sister who lived in another state and told her what had happened. Her sister became angry and said God did not do that, and that her sister had better have nothing else to do with that college, and then hung up. The phone awakened Lynn very early the next morning and it was her sister, who was crying. While her sister was brushing her teeth, she saw a sparkle and on closer inspection found that all her dark fillings were gold.

Remember Kathleen of the eight gold fillings? Her husband Jim was at work that Wednesday, and in the afternoon he felt a strange sensation in his mouth. He looked in the mirror and all his dark fillings had turned gold.

On Friday and Saturday of that week, I was in West Virginia introducing the bible college to interested churches. When the last session ended on Saturday afternoon, I briefly spoke about what was happening to us and invited anyone who was interested to stay and hear more. Twelve people remained behind. The sessions were held in the civic center. It was a mild day, the doors were open, and people on the street could see into the room. I spoke about some of the gold miracles and asked if they would like to pray. I had brought along my flashlight and dental mirrors, just in case. After the prayer, two people had gold fillings (both were Methodists). They were very excited and everyone was laughing and crowding around to see the gold. Several people were standing in the door watching, and I heard a woman say, "They must be dental students!"

Jesus Christ never changes. If you will let your faith touch Him, the miracles you are reading about will happen to you!

Chapter 4

I was invited to speak at a church closely linked with Cornerstone because they wanted to hear about and see what we were beginning to call "the tooth miracles". It was the Sunday morning service and the church was full. I had been a little unsure about what to do – should I try to find scriptures about miracles, signs and wonders that would fit, or should I just start at the beginning and simply tell what had happened? I chose the later, not knowing that this would become the format I would use in many churches.

I related everything from the very beginning, and I have never spoken to such an interested audience. When I finished speaking, we prayed and followed the steps that we had learned from Toronto Airport Christian Fellowship. Since it is impossible to check one's own mouth, we had a friend look before prayer to check for fillings or gold which a dentist may have placed. After the prayer the same person checked the fillings again. It is hard to describe the feeling that was in the room...it was charged with anticipation, excitement, anxiety, hope, and faith. The prayer had hardly finished when people began running to the front. One of the deacons had an entire tooth turn gold, and one of the pastors got a gold filling. The choir director got gold fillings, and while we were looking at the fillings, gold spread over a bottom molar – a beautiful crown! Everyone wanted to see and everybody was talking, laughing, and crying. I remember thinking that I could have left and no one would have noticed. We never got an exact count of the people who received gold, since one deacon was counting the number of people and another was counting the number of teeth that had changed. The last clear count I heard was that 13 people had received gold in their mouths.

We had amazing reports the entire week following the service. Almost all of the people who received miracles went home and showed family members, neighbors and friends. Some prayed for them to experience what they had experienced and it happened. To some it happened without prayer. Others called family and friends and it happened while they were talking. A woman named Linda had all her dark fillings turn gold, and when she got home she called her out of town family and several of them had the miracle happen without prayer. THIS IS MIND BOGGLING...IT HAPPENED ON THE TELEPHONE!!

Jesus Christ never changes. If you will let your faith touch Him, the miracles you are reading about will happen to you!

Chapter 5

I am the senior pastor of Cornerstone, the dean of the bible college, and I oversee the churches we have planted. Over the years, I have traveled some, spoken at conferences and in other churches, but not extensively. Our elders and I have believed that God would open the doors He wanted us to walk through, so I never passed out cards, asked if I could come and speak or did anything to open doors for myself. It is amazing how some of the invitations came, the following one for instance.

I have a friend named Dee whose home is in upstate New York. In the autumn, she would bring me wonderful antique apples with names I had never heard before from a special orchard near her home. I would always say, "Next year I'm going with you." I finally got it on my calendar and we were going up on Wednesday, pick apples, stay overnight in a quaint bed and breakfast and return home on Thursday. A week before the trip Dee had a call from her brother asking her if she knew any of the people who were experiencing the gold. Of course, she told him about me and said I'd be in their area in a few days. He asked if I'd be willing to meet with his pastor and talk about the possibility of later meetings. I was very reluctant to agree, as I was looking forward to a relaxing drive and beautiful scenery. I did not want to get dressed up and have a meeting. I agreed, however, and a time and place was set for dinner with the pastor prior to his mid-week service.

The scenery and the apples were more than I had anticipated, and we made it to dinner only a few minutes late. The pastor and his wife were very charming and gracious people, and it wasn't long before we were chatting like old friends. About twenty minutes into the conversation, he asked if I would speak that evening at his church, and I heard myself saying, "I'd be happy to!"

The service had already started when we arrived; the praise was joyful and you could sense currents of excitement. I had already decided that since I had been given no time to prepare that I would just talk about the tooth miracles.

The church was full and I noticed that the pastor did not sit down after he introduced me. He stood against the wall near the front, where a lot of young people and children were sitting on the floor. I remember that a storm was in progress and the lightening crackled through the P.A. system. I think there was hail also, but no one paid attention to the storm as I began to tell about the gold miracles we had seen. There was a lot of laughter and a lot of tears.

When I asked who wanted to pray for gold in their mouth, everyone's hand went up. After I had explained how we were going to proceed, there was such a joyous hubbub as mouths were examined. I asked the pastor to come pray for the miracles, and he was no sooner finished than his wife began jumping up and down. She had a beautiful gold filling that had not been there minutes before. Other people had gold, but somehow we never did get a count and I am reluctant to write about what cannot be verified.

After the excitement died down a little, I started to pray for individuals for healing. The fourth person in line was a young boy whose name was Josh. He smiled broadly and said, "Look!" I could see that his teeth were crooked, and he said, "I'm supposed to get braces but my family is too poor. Do you think Jesus will fix my teeth?" I said, "Yes…do you think He will?" He replied, "Yes, will you ask Him?" I laid my fingers on his lips and said, "Jesus, please make these teeth straight." I thought he would wait to see if the prayer was answered, but as soon as I said Amen, he ran off. I moved on to pray for the next person in line. A few minutes later, I heard a lot of noise. I looked up and Josh was running and jumping down the aisle surrounded by a swarm of kids. He pushed aside the person I was praying for and said, "Look!" He gave me a big smile and his teeth were perfectly straight! I found out later that the reason he had run off was to go look in the mirror to see what had happened. I cannot describe the excitement and joy that filled that place. Much, much later when I finally was settled in my room, I was not able to sleep for the joy and the awe of what I had seen.

Jesus Christ never changes. If you will let your faith touch Him, the miracles you are reading about will happen to you!

Chapter 6

I was working with a large church in North Carolina to help them establish a bible college. Right in the midst of the tooth miracles, I had a call from one of the pastor's assistants inviting me to speak at the annual Pastor's Appreciation Banquet. I was surprised because I knew it was customary for the speakers to be friends of the pastor. I had met with him several times, but certainly had no close association. I expressed my surprise to the woman with whom I was talking and she was very candid. Everyone they had wanted was unavailable, and I was a last resort. I was free at the time so I agreed to be the speaker. I was beginning to believe that maybe someone besides me was responsible for my engagements.

I was assigned a topic and told that my address should not exceed thirty minutes. I felt strongly that I should call the pastor and ask if he would like me to talk about the miracles instead of the assigned speech, but every time I called, I was referred to an associate. The day of the banquet arrived and I still had not talked to him. The formal affair was held in a hotel ballroom, and a gracious person picked me up at my hotel room. When I arrived at the ballroom, I was shown to a private sitting room where I remained until the dignitaries lined up to enter. I was seated next to the pastor who was receiving best wishes from many people. When the meal was served, he turned his attention to me and we began to talk. I told him that I was ready with a fine speech that I had written, but I would like to tell him some of the things that were happening to us. I shared several little stories with him. I noticed tears on his cheeks, so I paused. He then shared with me the most amazing thing, saying: "My church is so crowded on Sundays that we're in violation of a number of city codes. Our new church will be ready in six months and we've already outgrown it. We will immediately go to multiple services, but if we don't have the supernatural power of God, we will cease to be." His next statement made my knees knock. "Leave your speech in your purse and just tell us the things you've been telling me." He also said that after my introduction he would tell the people what he had asked me to do.

I have often thought that there could be no less likely place to see the Glory of God in tangible form. Here were hundreds of beautiful, elegant people in a secular setting with none of the things we think are necessary to bring such Glory. I began to tell the stories, and I noticed that the hotel staff was listening as they filled water glasses and poured coffee. It wasn't long before the staff stood against the back wall with their eyes fixed on me. I don't know how much time passed, but I suddenly remembered that I'd been given only thirty minutes. I said, "I think I may have exceeded my time." All over the room, people stood and spoke. I looked at the pastor who told me to please continue. When I couldn't think of another testimony, I asked if they'd like to pray for tooth miracles and there was very loud affirmation. I explained how we would proceed, and after everyone had their mouth checked, I asked the pastor to come and pray for the miracles. Having the pastor pray was to become standard practice for I felt it would make the miracles belong to the place where they happened instead of being connected to me.

It would be impossible to tell everything that happened after that meeting. Because the following day was Saturday, the church office wasn't open, but the pastor's home was flooded with so many calls and visitors that he had to call his staff in.

It was weeks before the reports stopped coming, but I will tell you two of my favorite testimonies.

A beautiful elderly man in a white tuxedo, walking with a cane with an ornate gold head, was brought to the front by his daughter. She said he was 83 years old and was very proud of the fact that he had all his teeth and he had never been to a dentist in his life. About a year ago, he had developed a cavity in a back molar that affected the entire tooth, but he refused to do anything about it. Both the man and his daughter were very excited and emotional because the entire tooth had turned gold, and as far as she could depress the gums with her fingernail, it was gold. When he went to the dentist for an x-ray, it appeared that both the tooth and the roots were gold. What an incredible thing that his first visit to the dentist at 83 years old was to verify a divine miracle!

A woman named Susan had her dark fillings turn gold and she could hardly wait to get home to show her husband, who was not a Christian. He became very upset and told her she could never go back to that church again because God did not do such things. He stormed out of the room and spent the night on the couch. At 6:30 the next morning, he awakened his wife and he was crying. While he was brushing his teeth, he discovered that every one of his dark fillings had turned brilliant gold. He is no longer an unbeliever, and guess where he goes to church?

Jesus Christ never changes. If you will let your faith touch Him, the miracles you are reading about will happen to you!

Chapter 7

Part of my work is to help strengthen the colleges we establish. I was teaching a three-day seminar at such a college in Pennsylvania, and I was invited to speak in the Sunday morning service of one of the churches the college serves. The seminar was very well attended, and although it was hard to stick to my subject, I managed to do so. Before the lunch break on the final day, I said that I would be devoting the last twenty minutes of the final session to something special. I spent the first ten minutes relating some of the miracles and then I asked if they would like to pray. A large percentage of the students were pastors, Methodists, Baptists, Lutherans, Pentecostals and Charismatics. Everyone participated, and two people immediately had gold appear in their mouths. A young woman had a crown turn gold, which almost completely covered her tooth. A Baptist pastor had his only filling turn a brilliant, beautiful gold. He kept asking, "Wow, why would God do that for me?" I had an excellent answer for him, "Because He loves you."

Word had spread about what happened in the seminar, and the host pastor asked me to share about the miracles in the Sunday morning service. The church was full and there was an air of excitement. Once again, I just related the miracle stories. Everyone was so attentive – everyone, that is, except one man (we'll talk about him later). The pastor's father, who had been a pastor for many years, was the first person to speak. It was his birthday, and he had received a beautiful gold crown. Several other people had gold fillings, and while we were looking at them (everybody in the building was crowding around trying to see), a woman came up the aisle dragging a young man whom I found out later was her son. He had broken a front tooth in an accident and had not yet had it replaced. It was broken off about half way up. His mother said she thought she saw the tooth move and gave him her compact mirror so he could see. We stood there in amazement and watched the tooth grow down. It is impossible to describe the feeling in that auditorium because many people knew him and knew about his broken tooth.

After the service, I was having lunch at the pastor's home, and we were interrupted by numerous phone calls with testimonies. The assistant pastor was driving home, and while stopped at a traffic signal he pulled down the visor mirror to look at his teeth. He discovered that all his dark fillings had turned gold! One woman had her mouth checked during the service, but nothing had happened. She lived with and cared for her mother in the next town, and while she was driving home, she kept thinking how encouraged her mother would be to see such miracles. They talked about the miracles when she got home, and her mother said, "Why don't you go look again?" She did and thought she could see a change, but wasn't sure. She asked her mother to check if the fillings were gold. Her mother looked and said, "Not all of the dark fillings are gold, some are silver." That was certainly an exciting phone call! The town's jeweler, who was also a gemologist, attended that church. After he looked at the gold teeth, the pastor asked him what he thought, and he said three words, "Awesome, awesome gold!"

Now, back to the man who was not attentive. I knew he had a problem with what I saying because he got up twice and went out. He also tried to sit in his chair in a way that he wouldn't have to look at me. At lunch I described him to the pastor, but he felt sure that the man didn't have a problem. At the next Sunday's service, the man asked if he could share something. Here is his story: He was very angry that his pastor would let "that woman" speak about such a subject in church. After the service, he talked to his wife about it all the way home and was so upset he couldn't enjoy his lunch. That evening while brushing her teeth, his wife discovered that all her dark fillings had turned gold. She called him to come look and pleaded with him not to be angry. He was so upset that he slept on the couch that night, and he had been asleep about an hour when he was awakened by a sensation in his mouth. He got up, looked in the mirror and found that one of his dark fillings had turned gold. At the top of each hour for the next seven hours, his seven remaining fillings turned gold. He said that the Army had done the original dental work and he had eight fillings.

Jesus Christ never changes. If you will let your faith touch Him, the miracles you are reading about will happen to you!

Chapter 8

∞

We are very close to a church in Georgia, and I was invited to speak at a camp for teenagers in January. It is unusual for me to be invited to speak to young people, and I was really looking forward to it. The camp was held in the country, and there were probably two hundred or more teenagers. On the opening night, there was a rock band concert and afterwards we had worship. The music during the entire weekend was jubilant.

We unloaded the car, settled in our rooms, and then I went to the cafeteria to chat with some of the kids. I had not been on the grounds very long when a young girl followed me into the ladies' room and asked if I would pray for her. She said she didn't want to wait until the service started. She showed me a tumor on the top of her wrist and said that she was scheduled to have a surgical procedure, but she wanted God to heal her. I prayed a simple prayer and she went back to her friends. This was Friday night.

Saturday was filled with classes and activities, and I spoke several times during that day and evening. Much time was given to praise and it was so good to see the teenagers dancing and jumping. On Saturday morning, the youth pastor said that they had not heard about the gold miracles and asked if I would please talk about them. I shared a few of the testimonies and asked if they would like to pray. Two of Cornerstone's elders were with me, and when we followed the procedure and looked into mouths, one of the elders had a beautiful gold crown. She said she was so intent on wanting the young people to see the miracles that she had not even considered that it was going to happen to her. We sat her down in a chair and had everyone come and look. All the kids responded joyfully.

In the service on Saturday night, two amazing things happened. During the praise time, the girl who had the tumor on her wrist danced up to me, stuck out her wrist and said, "Look it's gotten a lot smaller!" Another girl felt something in her mouth during the praise time, had her friend look at it, and discovered that she had a multi-colored filling that looked like part silver and part gold. Later, when she went to her dentist, he verified that it was gold and platinum. On that Saturday evening, it was very hard to stop the praise.

On Sunday morning, I went into the city to speak in the morning service of the church that had invited me. When I returned to the camp, a swarm of kids came running to meet my car and said that the tumor on the young woman's wrist

You're Kidding, Right?

had greatly decreased during the night.

There was a couple waiting to talk to me who introduced themselves as parents of one of the teenagers. Their daughter had an injury to her hand some months ago; the corrective surgery had not worked as well as they had expected and more surgery was scheduled. I do not even remember the girl, but on Friday night, she had apparently come up for prayer for her hand. The hand was totally healed and verified by the surgeon when she returned home.

By Sunday night, the praise was unstoppable. I'll never forget seeing so many young people twirling and dancing. We had tried twice to stop the praise and go on with teaching, but we couldn't. About an hour after the praise started, the girl with the tumor on her wrist danced by me, held out her wrist and said, "It's completely gone!" We had everybody come and look at it, and there was no indication that anything had ever been on her wrist.

Another thirty minutes went by and we were still caught up in praise. Several young people came up to me and said, "There's a fish in the sky above the lake." We were all in such an ecstatic state that I didn't respond. After at least ten kids talked to me about the "fish" in the sky, a Cornerstone elder came and said that he thought I should come and see. We stopped the praise and had everybody go outside. The camp fronted a lake, and stretching from horizon to horizon was a huge salmon. I did not know it at the time, but that elder has a college minor in climatology and had served 27 years in the Navy flying in various types of aircraft. He was quite used to, and well acquainted with the variety of cloud types, their altitudes and cloud movement. This is his analysis of what we saw:

"Eva, you asked for my analysis of what I saw when the kids said that they saw a 'fish' in the sky. As I told you, I have seen many clouds that assume various shapes as they are created, move and dissipate. The evening was a typical cold, clear (CAVU) night without any clouds or overcast. The stars and moon were out and it was quite bright. This cloud was unusual in that it was very high – 35-40,000 feet or higher. Since it was early January, the clouds had to be very high in order for the sun to still illuminate them at 8:00 p.m., as the sun sets about 5:15-5:30 p.m. My initial thought was, 'What a neat jet contrail.' But, after looking for a second I realized that it did not have the linear characteristics of a jet contrail, it had a very definite beginning and end, and was not linear. It was obviously fat – like a salmon. Secondly, the cloud stretched over approximately 60-70 percent of the sky, which was visible from horizon to horizon, and was moving from northwest to southeast – not an unusual direction for cloud movement. The fish was correct side up, traveling slowly in the same direction as the fish's nose and was obvious to everyone there. The shape was that of a very large salmon (or super-sized trout), and all fins were in the appropriate places – dorsal, pectoral, etc. The cloud was in perfect uniform contrast from nose to tail, and even the gill plates were in the correct anatomical location; all the scales were angled correctly toward the tail, as were the fins and tail. I thought, 'OK, let's wait a second and see what this cloud morphs into,' but it did not change as it proceeded over the full arc of the sky and was still wholly recognizable as a salmon as it headed over the southeast horizon. It was interesting that we were located approximately 50 miles west of Atlanta International Airport, the major hub of air traffic over the southeastern US, and during the period of time the 'fish' was visible, there was not one contrail visible anywhere in the sky. Later, plenty of contrails were visible going in various directions." (End of report.)

Being in a controlled atmosphere and seeing such miraculous events birthed tremendous faith in every person at the conference, and that faith will strengthen our lives forever. Since the time of that camp, the youth group in that church has grown greatly.

Jesus Christ never changes. If you will let your faith touch Him, the miracles you are reading about will happen to you!

Chapter 9

∞

I have mentioned before that many times it seemed that I wasn't the person who would decide where I would go. The following is a perfect example:

A long-time friend who pastors in Florida invited me to come share about the gold miracles with his congregation and other churches he was connected to. Since it wouldn't be out of my way, the church in Georgia (from Chapter 8) asked me to speak at their mid-week service on Wednesday. On the afternoon that I was to arrive, Sandy, the pastors wife, had a call from a friend who asked if she knew anything thing about a woman named Eva Evans. Sandy replied that I was on my way at that moment and would be speaking in the service that night. When Sandy's friend heard that, she said she didn't know anything about me but my name just kept coming to her. She thought that I should speak at their woman's conference later that year, which I did, and I will tell about that conference in a later chapter.

The Wednesday night service was wonderful, the presence of Jesus was very real, and there was a remarkable prophetic outpouring. The miracle I remember most was a word of knowledge that there was a man in the congregation who had colon cancer and was to have surgery soon. I was told later that he responded to the word of knowledge and believed that he was healed. He did, however, keep his appointment at the hospital, but when they went to perform the surgery, the tumor had disappeared! I spoke briefly about the gold miracles and didn't pray for them to happen.

The next evening I was invited to talk and pray with the worship team and musicians after their practice. My team and I arrived early so we could hear the praise. We had been there no more than twenty minutes when a woman came running to where I was sitting, opened her mouth, pointed and said, "What am I supposed to do about this?" It looked like her teeth were covered in gold! She seemed very agitated and went on to say, "I'm not even a member of this church. I was just visiting because I heard there was a special speaker. How could this happen? What am I supposed to do about it? I'm on my way to the airport to pick up my daughter, what am I supposed to tell her?" I started to laugh and people came over to see what was happening. When I was finally able to respond, I told her that she needed to go to her dentist immediately, have him verify that it was gold and get a copy of her records to show that he didn't put the gold in her mouth. She said, "Why would God do this for me?" I answered, "Because

He loves you and it made Him happy to give you a miracle!"
Jesus Christ never changes. If you will let your faith touch Him, the miracles you are reading about will happen to you!

Chapter 10

It was so great to be with my friends in Florida since we have been closely connected for years. The first service was Sunday morning, and the air was static with excitement and anticipation. With talented musicians and amazing worshipers, the service could go nowhere but up.

After I was introduced, I found myself once again telling the simple stories of the gold miracles we had seen. I had been speaking a short time when I noticed a man sitting in the front row with gold dust sparkling on his face and clothes. I stopped speaking for a moment, had him stand up so everyone could see the gold dust, and then went back to telling about the miracles.

We always used the pattern that we learned from Toronto Airport Christian Fellowship. After we prayed, everyone was looking for the gold, but there was none. We then moved into ministry and were praying for the needs of the congregation.

About twenty minutes later, a young man came running through the front door of the church – he and his wife both had gold fillings. They were in the car getting ready to leave when he pulled down the mirror on the visor and saw that he had three beautiful gold fillings and his wife had two gold fillings. Everyone was crowding around them to see the gold, and it sparked a chain reaction. I never did get an accurate count of how many people got gold in their mouths that morning!

At the Sunday night service there was standing room only. The first miracle we experienced that night related to me. As we were driving to the church, I kept wiping my hands with Kleenex because I thought I had used too much hand lotion. After a very joyful praise service, I was still wiping off what I thought was too much hand lotion. When I began to speak, I realized it was not hand lotion at all, but it was oil that was pooling in the palm of my right hand. I stopped speaking and showed the pastor. He said that I should anoint everyone that wanted to be anointed with the oil. I don't know the exact number of people I touched, but after I touched the last person waiting in line the oil just disappeared. I don't get the oil often, but I have had it several times since that night, and I always feel that it is for healing.

We have no verified record of how many people received gold in their mouths during that particular service since there were many visitors. In addition to the gold, one woman, who was partially blind, testified to having her eyes healed during the praise service. I remember her because she was dancing and whirling around, and I thought I had never before seen such large beautiful eyes. I went over to her and said, "You have such beautiful eyes." She answered, "Yes, they have just been healed!" It was the wee hours of the morning before we were able to leave.

The last meeting was on Monday evening, and again it was standing room only. The pastor told me that there had been many calls to his office that day asking for directions to the meeting. Although we had decided to make a concerted effort to get names and addresses of the people who had received miracles, it was impossible because of the crowding and all attention was focused on what God was doing. I believe that even though it was not verified, it would be safe to say as many as thirty people had received gold in their mouths. It's hard to explain what that service was like. If there were any skeptics there, they were not apparent. It seemed as if everyone there wanted and believed for a miraculous touch. I did not speak much that night; I simply told what God had been doing. Spontaneously, the miracles began to happen even before we prayed. The pastor, his staff and elders, and I were trying to determine just how many people did receive miracles when I heard a man say to a woman beside me, "Do you mind if I look?" He took a small flashlight out of his pocket and said, "Open, please." I asked if he was a dentist, and he replied, "Yes." He said he had heard what was happening and wanted to see it for himself. I asked what he thought, and he said it was the most beautiful gold he had ever seen.

On Tuesday evening, our friends took us to a church

several towns away. Early that morning, a member of my team came to my room and said that the Lord had given her a prophetic word for that church and had also told her that in that evening's service He would release the gold of Ophir. We were excited all day just talking about what we had already seen – we couldn't imagine how anything could be greater. The church was large and most of the people had not even heard about this kind of miracle. When I began to speak, they were very polite and gracious, but you could see that they were a little hesitant to be involved. So, once again, I just told the stories. As I spoke, I noticed that the teenagers and children began to filter back from classes, as did the teachers and nursery workers – everyone wanted to hear. When I finished speaking and asked if they wanted to pray for the gold, they were still very hesitant. I teased a little and said, "Oh, it won't hurt, it wouldn't be embarrassing." They reluctantly agreed, and we prayed a simple prayer. The first person to be checked was the father of the pastor's wife. He had an upper bridge and four dark fillings, and it looked like the upper part of his whole mouth was overlaid with beautiful sparkling gold. Everyone came to look at the gold, and even the small children were excited and involved. Again, because of the number of people, it was difficult to determine the number of miracles that happened that night. I personally was able to verify six additional miracles.

I have heard from so many people who received gold how it changes their lives forever. Almost every one of them comments on how close to God it makes them feel.

Jesus Christ never changes. If you will let your faith touch Him, the miracles you are reading about will happen to you!

Chapter 11

In Chapter 9, I talked about the pastor's wife who had called my friend Sandy about believing that I was to come to Florida for their annual women's conference. When she spoke with me and we prayed about it, we felt that it was very positive and that I should go.

The conference was held in a very large beachfront hotel. As has happened many times, I did not know anyone at the conference except my ministry team, and I had never seen the pastor's wife, Kay. We arrived in the early afternoon, and an hour or so later Kay came to speak with us. I always like to understand what the church leadership expects or wants, and even though they knew we had been involved in miracles, I had a feeling that they were not aware of the types of miracles, or to what extent we were involved. Kay had brought several of the church leaders with her to my room and we chatted for a while. Then I asked if she was fully aware of the types of miracles that we were seeing…she was not. So, without going into a lot of detail, I mentioned gold dust, gold teeth, other tooth miracles and miraculous healings. I asked her if that was their expectation for this conference. I could see that she was a little uncertain, so I told her one of the greatest truths I had learned about miracles: "The way this always seems to work is that when we talk about them, they happen, and when we don't talk about them, they usually don't happen." I told her it was a total dependence on faith and God. She thought a moment, looked at the women who were with her and said, "We would like to have miracles."

Before the conference began, my team and I spent some time walking on the beach and exploring the hotel. I was concerned that a karaoke bar was very close to the ballroom where we were meeting and thought it very likely that we might be disturbed by all the noise. Aside from that, everything seemed okay. The church had sent one of their best worship teams and soon we were so engrossed in worship that I forgot our surroundings. About forty minutes into the praise, someone came up to the worship leader and pointed out that there was gold dust all over the carpet on one side of the room. The gold dust was so profuse that people were scooping it up in napkins or handkerchiefs to take home. When it was my time to speak, I again told wonderful gold testimonies and we prayed for miracles. One woman immediately had a beautiful gold filling. Elation spread throughout the room and everyone was so involved in what was happening. After we looked at the tooth, it seemed that the right thing to do was to go back into the praise. During that time, a woman came over and asked if I would look at her mouth. She said that she had been born with a deformed mouth and had never been able to close her mouth with her teeth together. Chewing was sometimes very painful because she would often bite her tongue or jaw. She then asked if I thought God would heal her, and I said, "Yes, I did." She didn't even ask for prayer...she just danced away. Another person got a gold filling and while we were looking at her filling, the woman with the deformed mouth came up, grabbed the microphone, and said, "Listen to this!" She then started to click her teeth together. She said that never in her life had she been able to do that. Since everyone in the room knew her, it created quite a sensation. Another phenomenon happened that night. In different parts of the room, women began to fall without having anyone lay hands on them. Remember that karaoke bar? At 11:15 a hotel manager came and said he was so sorry to interrupt us, but our music was so loud it could be heard throughout the hotel!

The last session of the conference was on Saturday morning and we spent most of the time hearing accounts of what had happened to us all the night before. From that sharing came an outpouring of love – people were weeping, asking for forgiveness, and broken relationships where mended. When it came time to leave, I felt that seeds of real revival had been planted in lives.

Although I had only been invited to speak at the conference, I had planned to stay over for the Sunday morning services. Before we left the conference to drive into the city, Kay came and said her husband wanted me to speak at the first service. I remembered him saying that the eight o'clock a.m. service was usually sparsely attended. The pastor had arranged for me to meet him in his office that morning. We chatted lightly for a few minutes and then he told me that the women had brought back such astonishing reports from the conference they felt it should be shared with the whole church. As we were walking from his office to the auditorium he said, "One other thing, we've never had a woman pastor speak here before."

The "sparse" first service was completely full of joyful, anticipating people. Before I spoke, the pastor gave me a very gracious introduction and asked for the woman with the deformed mouth to come and tell what had happened to her. She and her husband had been with the church for many years and were well know to the congregation. She told what had happened and clicked her teeth together. Her husband said that the first time he had ever seen her eat normally was at breakfast that morning. The pastor also had someone come and talk about the gold dust on the floor at the conference. The pastor turned to where I was sitting and asked if I would please speak at the eleven o'clock service. Of course, I agreed and had a captive audience. There was so much laughter because many of the stories I related were very humorous. When I asked if they wanted to pray for mouth miracles, almost everyone in the auditorium stood up, and when we checked mouths, eight people had gold fillings! Those who had an opportunity to look into the mouths were just as excited as the people who received the gold fillings.

If such a thing was possible, the second service was even more exciting than the first. At the conference, one of the pastor's wives had told me that her parents, who were unbelievers, where going to be at the second service. She said she was a little nervous because they had never had experience with miracles. I knew who they were because they sat with her on the front row and seemed to be just as interested in what I was sharing as everyone else. After we prayed and looked for gold, I saw the wife look into her husband's mouth and then she screamed. Everyone started gathering around him and someone came and told me that he had received two beautiful gold crowns. He was not behaving at all like an unbeliever. It happened that a dentist who was a member of the church was at the second service. The pastor asked him if he would please check mouths, and after looking into a few, he said that never in his wildest dreams did he think he would be checking for and verifying supernatural fillings. In addition to the gold mouth miracles, sick people spontaneously came to the front for prayer. During that time, the pastor asked if I would please speak in the Sunday evening service.

Wonderful reports were told in that service. Several people said that they were going to make appointments with their dentists as soon as they could; others testified of being healed. I remember so clearly and often think about a group of very young children who had been released from the nursery. They came up to the front of the church and were sitting and playing on the steps that lead to the platform. Kay interrupted me and asked if I would come with her for a moment. We walked over to the children, I'm guessing there were about fifteen or sixteen, and every one of them had gold dust on their faces. More than one looked like they had a gold "milk mustache."

Jesus Christ never changes. If you will let your faith touch Him, the miracles you are reading about will happen to you!

Printed in the United States
16662LVS00001B/241-1050